Dr. Martin Luther King, Jr., THE PROPHET OF LOVE

TABLE TALK SERIES | VOLUME TWO

DAVID M. LOCKHART

Dr. Martin Luther King, Jr., The Prophet of Love
Copyright © 2021 by David M. Lockhart
All rights reserved. This book or any portion thereof may not be reproduced or used in any manner whatsoever without the express written permission of the publisher except for the use of brief quotations in a book review.

Limits of Liability and Disclaimer of Warranty
The author and publisher shall not be liable for your misuse of this material. This book is strictly for informational purposes. The purpose of this book is to educate and entertain. The author and publisher do not guarantee anyone following these techniques, suggestions, tips, ideas, or strategies will become successful. The author and publisher shall have neither liability nor responsibility to anyone with respect to any loss or damage caused, or alleged to be caused, directly or indirectly by the information contained in this book. Views expressed in this publication do not necessarily reflect the views of the publisher.

Cover Design: Designs by Triv (ilovedesignsbytriv@gmail.com)

Printed in the United States of America

Keen Vision Publishing, LLC
www.keen-vision.com
ISBN: 978-1-948270-82-3

To my father, the late Maxie Allen Lockhart, and my mother, Secemonia Miller Lockhart. Thank you for teaching me to treat everyone with dignity and respect. I could not have become the man I am today without my parents, who, through their life, showed and taught me never to give up and how to bounce back from adversity.

"Every man must decide whether he will walk in the light of creative altruism or in the darkness of destructive selfishness."

-Dr. Martin Luther King, Jr.

TABLE OF CONTENTS

Foreword by Chaplain (Colonel) US Army,
Retired Rodney A. Lindsay 7
The Table Talk Series Preface 9
Introduction 11
Chapter One
Dr. King's Background 19
Chapter Two
Dr. King's Trial Sermon of Love 23
Chapter Three
The Call and the Presence of God 27
Chapter Four
Dr. King Answers the Prophetic Call 31
Chapter Five
Dr. King Practices Nonviolent Love 35
Chapter Six
Agape Love 39
Chapter Seven
Violence Needs Agape Love 43

Chapter Eight
Dr. King's View of Love 47
Chapter Nine
The Conclusion 51
About the Author 55
Acknowledgments 57
Bibliography 59
Stay Connected 63

FOREWORD

There is no doubt that Dr. Martin Luther King, Jr. was a drum major for peace and justice, however, David M. Lockhart makes an undisputable case that Dr. King was a prophet of love which is the greatest of all human morals and values. Now abides faith, hope and love, but the greatest of these is love (First Corinthians 13:13).

This book lays out numerous examples of unconditional love that inspires the disfranchised, dispossessed, and the disinherited to boldly stand against injustice in a nonviolent way through civil disobedience. Dr. Martin Luther King is the epitome of the wise words of Frederick Douglass who stated that "there is no progress without a struggle."

In this book, David brilliantly and meticulously paints a portrait of Dr. King as a man of deep conviction and principle driven by the power of love. He demonstrates how Dr. King exudes radical changes and revolution that challenged and changed the consciousness of America.

David masterfully crafted a portrait of King who was highly motivated and driven to pursue justice and equality as witnessed by his unswerving commitment to civil rights not only African Americans but for all people.

Rodney A. Lindsay
Chaplain (Colonel) US Army, Retired

The Table Talk Series

PREFACE

The summer of 2017, a seminary trip to the Pilgrimage of Alabama Civil Rights Movement, a Doctoral Immersion Experience of the Civil Rights Movement, led us to Birmingham, Montgomery, and Selma, Alabama. It was a very enlightening journey. It was there I realized how little I knew about the Civil Rights Movement and the people who played an enormous part in the movement. I had to write an essay on a Civil Rights figure, and was inspired to do my essay on Fred Shuttlesworth; I wanted to know more about him. Upon the completion of the seminary project, I decided to turn that essay into the first volume of what would soon become the Table Talk Series.

The Table Talk series is designed to educate readers on the impact many unsung heroes had on the Civil Rights Movement. I envision the content of the series as perfect conversations for table talks when families and friends get together before or after dinner.

Knowledge without action is like a well-written book left unopened on a shelf; it doesn't benefit anyone. In this series, I provide knowledge to some and, perhaps, reignite the knowledge in others. My hope is that you will find yourself in several pages of this book, and that it leaves you with a passion to share with others.

As you prepare to dig in, I would like you to ponder the following questions:

- What is your long term strategy for your community?
- What reform do you perceive needs to take place in your community?
- What current projects are you working on with your community?
- How can you raise social awareness and increase participation in your community?
- How can we engage all races in the Civil Rights Movement in our communities?

There are many possible answers to the above questions. It is my sincere hope you find yours and implement them in your community. Thank you for sitting at the table with me. I hope this **Table Talk** is both enlightening and helpful.

"Whatever affects one directly, affects all indirectly. I can never be what I ought to be until you are what you ought to be. This is the interrelated structure of reality."

INTRODUCTION

The Civil Rights Movement had a tremendous impact on my life and the lives of all African Americans. It protested against racial segregation and discrimination, as well as economic, political, and social injustices. I would not be able to enjoy the liberty and justice that the Constitution promises if there had been no struggle for my legal rights.

The struggle for civil rights had a profound influence on me and my worldview. The demand for nonviolence, with its roots in peace, provided me with a framework for dealing with injustice in my life and the lives of those to whom I provide spiritual care.

I was not born in 1955 when officers in Montgomery, Alabama arrested Rosa Parks for refusing to obey a bus driver's demand that she give up her seat, in the black section of the bus, to a white person.

The driver asked her to give up her seat, in accordance with the law, because there were no vacant seats in the white section of the bus. My parents and their parents were born and raised in Alabama; they passed on the stories of the struggle for civil rights to me through oral tradition. They told and retold the civil rights stories and interpreted and revised them to help us preserve our sense of peace and endurance when we encountered prejudice and injustice.

The most powerful memory of the Civil Rights Movement was the death of Dr. Martin Luther King, Jr., when I was nine years old.

I was born in 1959, and, in 1968, Dr. Martin Luther King, Jr. was assassinated. When he died, my world and that of my family, faith community, and neighborhood stood still. Though I was young, I understood the impact of his death on the future of African Americans.

After the death of Dr. Martin Luther King, Jr., I became aware of the Ku Klux Klan and its mission to prevent African Americans from experiencing civil rights by using the most violent means possible: lynchings, burnings, and bombings. I never saw Ku Klux Klan members in person, but I saw pictures of them in newspapers, in magazines, and on television.

Some of my memories of the violence against activists surface when I reflect upon the movement. The violence against the Freedom Riders, both black and white, was a shameful, unforgettable occurrence in Alabama's history. Remember, the Freedom Riders rode buses across the south to protest against segregationists. They were often confronted and beaten.

Introduction

One of my memories of the Civil Rights Movement that always energizes me is Dr. Martin Luther King, Jr.'s "I Have A Dream Speech." In his speech, Dr. King said, *"I have a dream that one day down in Alabama — with its vicious racists, with its Governor having his lips dripping with the words of interposition and nullification — one day right there in Alabama, little black boys and black girls will be able to join hands with little white boys and white girls as sisters and brothers."*

The Civil Rights Movement was the American historical era that strategically transformed the judicial and legislative branch from discriminatory and unjust policies into legislation that prioritized equality in voting, the integration of schools, and the right to public resources. Before the Civil Rights Movement, the state and federal laws did not agree with the Fourteenth and Fifteenth Amendments to the Constitution. The Fourteenth Amendment guaranteed equal protection under the law for all people. The Fifteenth Amendment stated that you could not deny a citizen the right to vote base on that citizen's race, color, or previous condition of servitude.

The Civil Rights Movement's strategy to transform America, employing nonviolent demonstrations and peaceful political protests, is impressive. The movement's use of civil disobedience, which entailed peaceful political demonstrations, was morally justified because of the "separate but equal" legal doctrine. Separate but equal was a policy that stated that if the facilities provided to each race were equal, state and local governments could require that services be segregated by "race." African American activists' employment of civil disobedience was unlawful to many of the powers in the south. But they exercised it with their consciences rooted in the biblical record, which affirmed humanity as having been created free and in the image of God, the Creator.

What impresses me most about the movement is that African Americans were willing to practice civil disobedience, knowing that the outcomes of disobeying the "separate but equal" law included jail time, the threat of bodily injury, and even the loss of life.

The Civil Rights Movement activists (many of who were of other races) were willing to give up their lives so that all human beings created in God's image could enjoy the same freedom as an "American." They were like those whom John spoke about when he said, *"No one has greater love than this, to lay down one's life for one's friends."* (John 15:1 NRSV) The leaders of the movement were activists who dedicated themselves to the cause, but the movement also included loyal followers who united and empowered the mission through their participation. The Montgomery Bus Boycott, which was under the leadership of Dr. Martin Luther King, Jr., displayed the unity of the movement. It was a successful protest that lasted 281 days.

The historical era of the Civil Rights Movement owes much to dedicated, brave, and loyal activists as well as African American citizens who understood the importance of unity and perseverance. Moreover, the

Civil Rights Movement was a momentous historic event because of lawyers who strategically filed legal actions and the National Association for the Advancement of Colored People's awareness of the need for these lawyers.

The Civil Rights Movement influenced my life and ministry profoundly, especially Dr. Martin Luther King, Jr. He did much more than speak peace. Dr. King displayed calmness in the face of violence, discrimination, prejudice, and injustice. He suffered to make a difference in the lives of his people. He gave his life so that others would experience equality. In my ministry, I encounter people who struggle with an array of issues and help them find solutions to those problems through coaching and counseling them to walk in peace and act in love.

The Bible proclaims, *"Love never fails."* (Romans 13:8) During the Civil Rights Movement, Dr. King demonstrated his enduring love for his brothers and sisters as well as his love for his enemies. He suffered under the yoke of nonviolence and became the embodiment of love that made the world a better place for African Americans, women, and other voiceless groups of people. In my ministry, I follow the example of Dr. Martin Luther King, Jr., as he followed Christ, knowing, *"Love never fails."*

Dr. King left behind a legacy of encouragement through his speeches and sermons. Rarely did he seek encouragement for himself. He utilized his communications to encourage others. Let us be that agent of change and love all our brothers and sisters regardless of race.

Dr. Martin Luther King, Jr., The Prophet of Love

Let there be change in the world, and let it begin with me.
Let there be change in the world, the change that must be.
Our God created us, brothers and sisters, we were all born free.
This is the truth that brings change. It's truth that sets us free.
Let there be change in all the earth, and let it begin with me.
Let there be change in the earth, the change that must be.
Our God created us in God's image. Our God created us free.
This is the truth that demands change. God created you and me.
Let there be peace in the universe, and let it begin with me.
Let there be peace in the universe. The peace that was meant to be.
With God as our Father, brothers and sisters are we.
Let there be peace in the universe. The peace that keeps us free.
Let there be celebration in all the earth, and let it begin with me.
I will always choose love over hate.

David M. Lockhart
Excerpt from sermon on Dr. Martin Luther King Jr.
penned in Iraq, 2010.

TABLE TALK

Reflect on the following questions and discuss them with others at the table.

- What are your memories of or experiences with the Civil Rights Movement?
- What were the pros and cons of the separate but equal policy?
- What does John 15:1 (NRV) mean to you?
- My framework for dealing with injustice is rooted in nonviolence. How do you deal with injustice?

"An individual has not started living until he can rise above the narrow confines of his individualistic concerns to the broader concerns of all humanity."

-Dr. Martin Luther King, Jr.

Chapter One

DR. KING'S BACKGROUND

Dr. Martin Luther King, Jr., born in 1932, was nurtured through the loving care of his parents and the Ebenezer Baptist Church to love God and neighbor.[1] In 1944, at the age of fifteen, he entered Morehouse College; he graduated in 1948. Dr. King graduated from Crozer Seminary in 1951, and was a Boston University doctoral graduate in 1955. However, before he graduated, he accepted Dexter Avenue Baptist Church's call to pastor this historic congregation. He began his pastoral walk in 1954,[2] following in the steps of his father, grandfather, and great-grandfather—Baptist preachers, who nurtured congregations to love God and neighbor.[3] Dr. King was the embodiment of God's love; he lived and died expressing that love in words and actions. The love of God consumed him as he answered the call to be the prophet to the world that God loved. Therefore, as a righteous man of God, he had to do as Henry David Thoreau proposed, *"Stand against the world's evil."* [4]

Seminary Vision of a Prophetic Ministry

In his book entitled: *Dream, Martin Luther King, Jr., and the Speech That Inspired a Nation*, Drew D. Hansen writes:

"Following Dr. King's activism, one of his seminary professors remembers Dr. King's perspicacious interest in the prophets of the Old Testament. While in seminary, Dr. King wrote an essay on the ministry of the prophet Jeremiah. He praises Jeremiah for resisting the status quo and condemns everyone, present, and future, who would not do the same. In Dr. King's view, championing the status quo, whether a church or an individual, is damaging to the Christian faith."[5]

While he was in seminary, Dr. King wrote another essay, reproving the author of a book for describing religion as nothing more than a declaration of what society finds valuable. In response to this author, employing the ministry of the prophet, Dr. King raised this question: What is the theory to explain a prophet's departure from society's values, lifting a standard that transcends the standard of humanity? Hansen argues that Dr. King thought about employing the prophetic vocation as a model for ministry during his seminary years.[6]

TABLE TALK

Reflect on the following questions and discuss them with others at the table.

- Henry David Thoreau proposed that we should "stand against the world's evil." What do you propose we should do to stand against the world's evil?
- Do you believe shaping our activism in nonviolence will be effective today?
- What does the phrase "employing the prophetic vocation as a model for ministry" mean to you?

"Love is the only force capable of transforming an enemy into a friend."

-Dr. Martin Luther King, Jr.

Chapter Two

DR. KING'S TRIAL SERMON OF LOVE

Charles Marsh, the author of the book, *The Beloved Community*, rightly asserted that the trial sermon Dr. King preached at Dexter, "The Three Dimensions of a Complete Life," had no signals that pointed to his futuristic activism. It was rooted in three ethical principles. The three principles that formed and shaped Dr. King's sermon were length, breadth, and height. When Dr. King spoke of length, he was referring to the length of life and the need to care for oneself. The second principle in his sermon was breadth. Dr. King understood breadth as existing outside oneself. In his understanding, breadth was caring about the needs of others. Height was the third principle in Dr. King's sermon; it pointed upward, referring to humanity's upward reach of God.[7]

Dr. King's trial sermon lacked indication of his future as an activist because Dr. King did not intend to become a civil rights activist. It was God's will, and not Dr. King's ambition, that led him down the path of activism. Jeremiah

1:5 says, *"Before I formed you in the womb, I knew you; Before you were born, I sanctified you; I ordained you a prophet to the nations."* Just like God knew Jeremiah had a special calling on his life, God knew that Dr. King had a special calling to be a future civil/human rights leader and spokesperson.

The Sermon's Second Principle

Without a doubt, Dr. King was not aware of his future activism when he preached his trial sermon. However, after close examination, the theme of love, which was the source of his activism, shone through the ethical principles communicated in his trial sermon. The second principle, breadth, would come to describe King's activism: reaching out to his neighbors and others to meet their needs. I contend it was love that empowered Dr. King to reach out to global neighbors in hopes that he could turn their lives away from racism, poverty, and war. When Dr. King preached his trial sermon, unconsciously, he preached of his future activism.

The Sermon's Third Principle

The third principle in Dr. King's trial sermon was height, referring to reaching up to God who is love. In his trial sermon, Dr. King was prophesying his future activism because only the love of God could carry him through the struggle for racial equality. Moreover, it would be God's love that would help him transform evil racism through his practice of nonviolent resistance.

TABLE TALK

Reflect on the following questions and discuss them with others at the table.

- Dr. King was a servant leader. What are some principles of a servant leader?
- How was Dr. King able to put God at the center of the Civil Rights Movement?

"I still believe that standing up for the truth of God is the greatest thing in the world. This is the end of life. The end of life is not to be happy. The end of life is not to achieve pleasure and avoid pain. The end of life is to do the will of God, come what may."

-Dr. Martin Luther King, Jr.

Chapter Three

THE CALL AND THE PRESENCE OF GOD

In his book, *Stride toward Freedom*, Dr. Martin Luther King, Jr. writes that he and his wife, Coretta, were excited about returning to the South. After they arrived in Montgomery, they were confident a transformation was coming to the South, and they wanted to take part in it. However, Dr. King continues to write, they were uncertain of how the transformation would come about and how they would participate in it. [8]

It was at the beginning of his call to love neighbor as self and serving as president of the newly-formed Montgomery Improvement Association (MIA) that Dr. King encountered God's presence with him in this new role. After Dr. King was appointed president of the newly formed MIA,[9] the day of the Montgomery boycott, a small group of leaders gathered to make plans for the mass meeting the same night. When the leaders' meeting ended, those present had less than an hour to dress and return to the church for the mass meeting. After arriving at his home, Dr. King told his wife, Coretta, that he had been elected the MIA president. She voiced her support as he embraced the call to be president of the MIA, even though they had agreed that he would limit his ministry to his new congregation upon arriving in the city. [10]

Dr. King experienced love and peace after Coretta embraced his new role. Therefore, knowing his wife was comfortable with his new leadership role, Dr. King went to his study to prepare his sermon for the mass meeting. However, noting the limited time he had to prepare, twenty minutes, he became nervous. Dr. King was overwhelmed with fear. He began to doubt himself; he lost his courage. He was troubled because the television cameras would be pointed at him, and newspaper personnel would record his words. The leaders who had elected him the speaker of the night did not tell him what to say, but he knew what the people needed to hear to continue in the struggle. But he did not feel adequate to communicate to the people guidance and instruction. It was at that moment that Dr. King reached up to God in prayer. He did not pray a long prayer, but he prayed a fervent, sincere prayer. Dr. King prayed that God would remove his nervousness and be present with him. He told God that he needed him at that moment more than he ever needed him before. [11]

After Dr. King prayed, he was no longer nervous; his emotions were no longer scattered and out of control. He became focused and confident with only fifteen minutes to prepare the most important sermon he had ever preached.

Reaching for a pad, he began to outline his speech. He was acutely aware that his speech had to be powerful enough to arouse the people to action but peaceful enough to deter the violence and resentment some were feeling. [12]

TABLE TALK

Reflect on the following questions and discuss them with others at the table.

- Why was it important for Dr. King to get his wife, Coretta, onboard before he was all in?
- What can you do to assert your faith and calm your fears so you can deal with the things that are causing you to be fearful?
- How do you get others to see the importance of prayer in leading change?

"The past is prophetic in that it asserts loudly that wars are poor chisels for carving out peaceful tomorrows."

-Dr. Martin Luther King, Jr.

Chapter Four

DR. KING ANSWERS THE PROPHETIC CALL

The Dexter Avenue Baptist Church appointed Dr. Martin Luther King, Jr., pastor of their historic congregation.[13] After arriving in Montgomery in 1955, King became an active member of the National Association for the Advancement of Colored People (NAACP), was appointed to various committees, and elected to various offices.[14] He also joined the Alabama Council on Human Relations soon after he joined the NAACP.[15] A major challenge of the NAACP was the shameful racism African Americans experienced while riding the buses in Montgomery. It was common for African Americans to pay at the front door and then walk to the back door to enter the bus. They didn't arrive at their destinations on time because before they could reach the door, the bus driver would pull off. The dime they paid to ride the bus was counted as a loss; it was not refunded.[16]

In 1955, after the arrest of a fifteen-year-old African American female, Claudette Colvin, there was much talk about boycotting the buses.[17] However, a few months later, on December 1, 1955, Rosa Parks, an African American seamstress, was arrested for not giving her seat to a white passenger; thus, the NAACP was compelled to act. The leaders who were compelled to protest by employing a boycott were E. D. Nixon, a railroad employer; Dr. King and Rev. Ralph Abernathy, pastor of Montgomery First Baptist Church. These three NAACP leaders contacted other ministers to attend a meeting to unite in boycotting Montgomery's buses. Mrs. A. W. West, the widow of an eminent dentist, contacted other civic leaders.[18]

The meeting was held at Dexter Avenue Baptist Church and was a tremendous success with most community leaders and ministers present. Another meeting was necessary to complete plans for the boycott. This meeting was held at Holt Street Baptist Church on December 5, 1955. The eighteen African American taxi companies in the city agreed to provide transportation to and from work at the bus rate: ten cents. The one-day boycott was successful, but it was a difficult day for some because also scheduled that morning was the trial of Rosa Parks. After noting empty buses passing his house, Dr. King rushed to the courthouse to witness the trial. The court determined her guilt and fined her ten dollars; she paid, but she also appealed.[19]

After the trial, around three in the evening, some of the leaders made plans for the mass meeting that night. In the meeting, they were aware of the need for an "improvised" organization, and thus, they formed a new organization.

They named it the Montgomery Improvement Association. Without warning, the group chose Dr. King to serve as president of the newly formed MIA.[20]

I contend that electing Dr. Martin Luther King, Jr., to serve as president of the MIA was God's call on his life to lead African Americans on the civil rights journey. I would further suggest that God called Dr. King to Montgomery through the call of the people of Dexter Avenue Baptist Church. Dr. King unconsciously came to Montgomery to resist the evil in the world and to stand against racism and injustice in Montgomery that would, over time, spread throughout the world to include Africa and Vietnam.

On one occasion, when Dr. King was sharing his story of activism, he made it clear that his history of activism was rooted in circumstance and not in ambition. He contended that his only reason for coming to Montgomery was to pastor Dexter Avenue Baptist Church. However, the racism inherent in discrimination against African Americans riding public transport compelled him to act. He made it clear that he did not start the activism, and neither did he insist on it; his involvement was sought. He became involved in the Civil Rights Movement in Montgomery, responding to the call of African Americans. They grew weary of constantly suffering under the weight of racism and injustice and needed a voice to resist the evil of white supremacy.[21]

TABLE TALK

Reflect on the following questions and discuss them with others at the table.

- Claudette Colvin was considered to be the forerunner for Rosa Parks and the Montgomery Boycott. What are ways each generation can be an effective frontrunner for generations to come?

- Can activism be woven effectively into the office of a pastor? Can a pastor serve them both without conflict?

- African Americans grew weary of the weight of racism and injustice and needed a voice to resist. How do we find our voice when we grow weary of societal ills?

Chapter Five

DR. KING PRACTICES NONVIOLENT LOVE

Dr. King was an intellectual who understood the importance of a framework to practice activism. His knowledge of the need for a framework caused him to revisit the theories of scholars he studied at the institutions of higher learning he attended, as well as the theories of others. He concluded that he agreed with the theory of the ethics of love employed by Gandhi. Gandhi employed nonviolent resistance to lead the successful campaign for India's independence from British rule. Gandhi's nonviolent resistance would be valuable to him in his struggle to free African Americans from racism and injustice. King studied Gandhi's ethics of love and was impressed with how Gandhi had transformed the principle. Before Gandhi, the ethics of love was limited to relationship building between two or more people, but Gandhi successfully employed the principle to institutions.[22]

Gandhi understood love's connection with nonviolence and social change. Gandhi's nonviolence theory was the social-reform strategy that Dr. King found most valuable for his activism.[23] It was a social-reform method that connected Dr. King to his three principles: length, breadth, and height. Dr. King's activism was offering himself (length) for others (breadth) through the empowerment of God (height).

Gandhi's theory of nonviolence that Dr. King embraced was twofold. The theory resisted the urge to hate a neighbor who practiced violence against you. It employed the spirit of love to free oneself from the soul's hatred and violence against a neighbor who practiced physical hatred and violence against you. If there was no hate in your heart for a neighbor who hated you, there was no hate in your heart to practice physical violence against your neighbor. It is senseless to harm a neighbor who practiced hatred against you but who you do not hate because the spirit within you is the spirit of love. Nonviolent resistance also withstood the urge to practice physical violence against a neighbor whose strategy was physical violence.[24]

Those who employed the strategy of nonviolence to free the oppressed from the oppressor understood the oppressed are formed and shaped into the image of the oppressor through tactics of resentment and acts of violence. The oppressed can find no value in resentment and acts of violence because love cannot rise out of hate. It is only through love that those who practice the evil of racism and hatred can transform and experience the enlightenment of love. Those who practice hate instead of love multiply hatred in the cosmos. When hatred multiplies in the cosmos, love diminishes. Those who are wise decrease the hate in the world by loving neighbor as self; with this, they transform the world. [25]

TABLE TALK

Reflect on the following questions and discuss them with others at the table.

- Why is it important to lay out a framework before speaking truth to power?
- Why was Gandhi's theory of nonviolence effective for Dr. King?
- Dr. King's activism was offering himself (length) for others (breadth) through the empowerment of God (height). How can we offer ourselves (length) for others (breadth) through the empowerment of God (height)?

"We must develop and maintain the capacity to forgive. He who is devoid of the power to forgive is devoid of the power to love. There is some good in the worst of us and some evil in the best of us. When we discover this, we are less prone to hate our enemies.."

-Dr. Martin Luther King, Jr.

Chapter Six

AGAPE LOVE

In his book *Stride toward Freedom*, Dr. King contends the love of nonviolent resistance is not emotional love but love rooted in an awareness of the human condition. It is love that promotes benevolence, kindness, and consideration until hatred transforms. Dr. King writes that an understanding of the different Greek meanings of the word love is valuable when explaining how to employ it in the practice of nonviolent resistance. In the Bible, the New Testament is in Greek, and there are three definitions of the word love, employing Platonic philosophy. [26]

In Greek, the word love can mean eros, if the focus of that love is God and craving in hope for the presence of God. However, Dr. King writes that the meaning of the word has transformed to define romantic love in this modern world. In Greek, when defining the love of friendship between individuals, the word is philia. The third meaning of the word love in Greek is agape; it defines love that seeks the good of neighbor, putting the needs and wants of neighbor first. The practice of nonviolent resistance employs agape love. Agape love resists the urge to practice violence against the neighbor who hates and, instead, shows goodwill toward the one who loves. It is the practice of agape love to display love equally to the unloving neighbor as well as the loving one. [27]

The agape love of nonviolent resistance insists that loving the neighbor who loves and hating the neighbor who hates is loving a neighbor who loves for a reward. If one loves the neighbor who is loving, the neighbor who is loving will respond. Therefore, the loving one extends to the neighbor who is loving is not genuine. However, if one loves the neighbor who practices violence and displays evil racism, the one who practices violence will not respond. The best strategy is to extend love to the neighbor who practices racism and injustice, knowing the neighbor who engages in these evil practices will not respond. The knowledge that love is not always genuine makes it necessary to love the neighbor who practices violence against you. Once you practice love against the neighbor who practices violence against you, knowing the neighbor will not respond, you can be certain that your love is agape.

The strategy of nonviolent resistance with its roots in agape love understands the need for loving the neighbor who practices violence against you as meeting the neighbor's needs. The neighbor who practices violence needs agape love to share in the love that builds and supports global citizenry. An example of the love that builds and supports global citizenry is visible in the story of the Good Samaritan (Luke 10:25–36). The Samaritan met a stranger who was beaten and naked as he journeyed. The stranger was traveling on Jericho Road without anyone to provide for his need. Jesus identified the stranger as a neighbor, even if the Samaritan did not know the stranger. The Samaritan encountered a neighbor with a need, and he graciously responded to that need in multiple ways.

When the Samaritan responded to those needs, the Samaritan became "the good Samaritan." The strategy of nonviolence insists on loving the neighbor who practices violence, knowing the neighbor who practices violence has a need that calls for an agape response. The strategy of nonviolence is the practice of meeting the needs of those who practice violence against you because agape love is not selective in the practice of love. The neighbor who practices violence against you needs the agape love that brings the neighbor into citizenry with those who increase love in the cosmos, thus decreasing hatred. [28]

TABLE TALK

Reflect on the following questions and discuss them with others at the table.

- The strategy of nonviolence insists on loving your neighbor who practices violence. Is this an effective strategy in today's society?

- Jesus identified the stranger on the Jericho road as a neighbor. What do you think is the significance of calling him a neighbor?

- Why was it necessary to place the word "good" before the Samaritan when he had already done a good deed?

Chapter Seven

VIOLENCE NEEDS AGAPE LOVE

When African Americans love neighbors who practice violence against them, they respond to European Americans' need for redemption. The agape love that African Americans extend to European Americans who practice violence against them is the love God extended to humanity when he sent his Son to die for humanity (Romans 5:8). In like manner, African Americans can love their European American neighbors who practice violence against them while European Americans are still sinners, practicing their violence of hatred and racism. While they are practicing violence against African Americans, they are most in need of the transforming love of nonviolence.

Due to the violence racist European Americans inflicted on African Americans, those European Americans are identified as abusive neighbors. These abusive neighbors practice racism and hatred with characters that blemish and wound by their love for segregation. Only the love of

African Americans can reform disfigured racist European American souls. African Americans must embrace the love of nonviolence to reform the souls of European Americans who practice racism and injustice. European Americans need the liberating love of African Americans to enlighten their souls to experience freedom from the anxiety, fear, and irritation that racism breeds.

The agape love African Americans extend to racist European Americans is not fragile and submissive but strong through movements and operations to create and preserve the agape citizenry. It demands living in agape love citizenry, regardless of the cost, situation, or circumstance. The agape love of nonviolent resistance will make sacrifices to bring peace out of chaos to restore citizenry. Agape love is resilient, refusing to break under the yoke of violence, practicing forgiveness whenever extended, and even when it is not.

The strategy of nonviolent resistance to restore citizenry is patterned after God's strategy to restore humanity's relationship with him through the death of Jesus on the cross. God paid a high cost to redeem humanity from the destruction of sin, which prevented humanity from taking part in citizenry. The greatest call to humanity is the call to share in citizenry. Humanity can continue to share in citizenry purchased on the cross through the presence of the Holy Spirit. God, who created, restored, and bought citizenry for humanity, is against those who work to bring disorder out of citizenry.

African Americans are guilty of bringing disorder out of citizenry if African Americans engage in violence against those who engage in violence against them. Those who work against citizenry, practicing racism and hatred, work against themselves because working against citizenry's love brings emptiness. The emptiness of isolation can never be filled without participation in citizenry.[29]

Booker T. Washington was an advocate for the practice of agape love, arguing for strength to resist being pulled down so low that you open yourself up to hate. He understood hatred was a powerful force that robbed oneself of dignity. Dr. King contends that those who lose their dignity under the low standard of hate are opposed to citizenry. The failure to understand love as the only means of participating in citizenry is the failure to understand the connectedness of being human. It is also the failure to understand all men and women are sisters and brothers. Love is the force that connects and preserves citizenry.[30]

TABLE TALK

Reflect on the following questions and discuss them with others at the table.

- Do you believe the love of African Americans can reform disfigured racism?
- What do you think is the strategy of nonviolence today? Do you believe there is a strategy that can establish authentic unity?

Chapter Eight

DR. KING'S VIEW OF LOVE

Dr. King's moral principles to guide the Civil Rights Movement centered on love. His focus on liberating African Americans and transforming America was love employed through nonviolence. The practice of nonviolence to combat the sufferings of the innocent was his moral thought. The strategy for Dr. King's ethical action was love. Studying the works of Paul Tillich shaped his understanding of the connectedness between love, power, and justice. When Dr. King spoke of power, he inferred that the power of love carried out the authority of justice. Dr. King believed that justice was love, making right all that opposed love.[31]

Love Triumphs in Montgomery

On Tuesday, November 13, 1956, while Dr. King was sitting in a Montgomery courtroom waiting to hear the court's decision on a city petition declaring the bus boycott illegal, a reporter, Rex Thomas, placed a sheet of paper in his hands. The United States Federal Court in Montgomery ruled bus segregation laws were in violation of the Fourteenth Amendment and were unconstitutional. It took thirteen months for Dr. King and other civil rights activists to champion Jim Crow laws that legislated and enforced racial segregation in the South.[32]

After the court decision that bus segregation was unconstitutional, Dr. King and the Civil Rights Movement leaders prepared the people for proper behavior on integrated buses. They informed other African Americans that winning civil rights to integrate the buses was not about African Americans winning and European Americans losing, but about living in a country where justice and democracy were not limited to a few.

Dr. King and other ministers who were leaders in the Civil Rights Movement in Montgomery prepared the people for riding integrated buses. The main emphasis was on understanding the passing of the law as a triumph for law and justice and not triumph over those who practiced racism and injustice. African Americans in Montgomery received materials to train and teach them acceptable and unacceptable behavior for full participation in integration. Dr. King also reached out to white clergy, suggesting they prepare their congregations for proper behavior when riding integrated buses. However, the white clergy did not respond to Dr. King's suggestion. The training Dr. King and other clergy leaders provided the Montgomery African American community included role-playing. [33]

Impact of the Love Triumph

The triumph of Montgomery inspired Dr. King to hope in a transformed America. In his book, *To Make the Wounded Whole*, Lewis V. Baldwin argues that Dr. King understood the Jim Crow South as the paradigm to transform America to bloom with flowers of democracy. It was also Dr. King's understanding that the injustices of racism African Americans experienced in the South paralleled with global injustices of racism. While African Americans in Montgomery were suffering under the weight of racism, third-world people strived for their liberation from oppression. After noting the similarities between the striving of African Americans and the third-world people, Dr. King acknowledged their commonality.[34]

Love Never Fails

In April 1968, someone assassinated Dr. King in Memphis, Tennessee. The world mourned the heartbreaking news of his death and responded with expressions of love, tributes, and condolences. There were multiple world councils, alliances, and national associations who mourned Dr. King's death and spoke of him as the beloved who was valiant in action and brilliant of mind. It was also the united consensus of all organizations that Dr. King was "a first citizen of the world." There were acknowledgments of Dr. King's activism from the London Times, the United Nations' secretary-general, Prime Minister Indira Gandhi, and many others.[35]

Love Triumphs.

Dr. King's love triumphs in his life and death. The tribute that raised love from grief and sorrow were the words of the Catholic Pope Paul VI. Pope Paul VI vowed that "the virtues of justice and international love" that Dr. King embodied would be honored and embraced worldwide. The words Pope Paul VI prayed came from his mouth, but Dr. King's heart of love. The prayer was an assurance that the love Dr. King expressed in words and actions would become a reality in all the world.[36]

TABLE TALK

Reflect on the following questions and discuss them with others at the table.

- Dr. King and the leaders of the Civil Rights Movement prepared the people for proper behavior. How do we prepare ourselves and generations for proper behavior when faced with injustice?

- Can you maintain a heart of love when you are surrounded by hate?

Chapter Nine

THE CONCLUSION

It was not difficult for Dr. King to step into a prophet's role because God called him to preach the gospel. It is the understanding of some theologians and scholars that the pastor's role includes prophetic and priestly roles. In this understanding, the role of the pastor is threefold: pastor, prophet, and teacher. Dr. King functioned well in all three. In his book, *I May Not Get There with You: The True Martin Luther King, Jr.*, author Michael Eric Dyson writes:

> *Dr. King's participation in the Civil Rights Movement thoroughly convinced his role of leadership was the call of God on his life.* [37]

Dr. King's sense of call empowered him to stand under unsurmountable hardships. The Montgomery Bus Boycott success inspired Dr. King to enlarge his vision, seeing in it the call of God to do greater works. He was a Civil Rights Leader with resiliency because he was certain the God who called him was in control of his life and destiny. I contend that this is the reason Dr. King had no fear of bodily harm from those he "resisted evil" to liberate neighbors from social injustice.

Was Dr. King a prophet? Marsh, like so many others, struggles to respond to this question. He is not certain of the call on Dr. King's life, but what he is certain of, he speaks. Marsh contends that if Dr. King was a prophet, he was not one because he prophesied to Americans words of transformation, inclusiveness, and justice. It is Marsh's conviction that if Dr. King was a prophet, it was because he sacrificed his life to embrace the call of God — loving neighbor as himself and believing in God's Holy Word. It is a Word that proclaims that the peace of the world came through Jesus.[38]

James Cones contends that Dr. King was a charismatic prophet who, through his prophecy, inspired the spirit of emancipation in the hearts of African Americans, preaching liberation theology.[39]

It is my argument that Dr. King was a prophet because, by speaking truth, he laid down his life for others, knowing it was the price he had to pay for speaking truth to power. He knew that speaking truth to power could cost him his life, yet he continued to speak because, like Jesus, God sent him into the world to love the world.

One of Dr. King's last missions was the Poor People Campaign that he didn't get the chance to see through before his assassination. His vision was to develop a strategy beyond demanding civil rights for African Americans to end poverty for all races.[40] Rev. Dr. William Barber, Pastor of at Greenleaf Christian Church in Goldsboro, North Carolina and founder of Repairers of the Breach, in his speech, "Walking in the Footsteps of MLK" at Stanford University, began by arguing against indulging in nostalgia for the glory days of the Civil Rights Movement.

"I'm humbled to stand before you as we honor the legacy of Rev. Dr. Martin Luther King, and I will tell you, I don't do King celebrations. Because I think we're at a point where we do not need to celebrate as much as we need to engage. To truly honor a martyr, we must go where they fell, pick up their baton, and carry it the rest the way."

The Rev. Dr. William J. Barber II and Rev. Dr. Liz Theoharis, co-chairs of the Poor People's Campaign, have picked up the baton to finish Dr. King's Poor People Movement Campaign.

God, we thank you for the selfless service of Martin Luther King Jr., who dreamed of an America free from injustice. We thank you for his commitment and courage, even to the point of death. We pray that we may exhibit such determination in our struggles and wherever we are called to fight for freedom.

TABLE TALK

Reflect on the following questions and discuss them with others at the table.

- Dr. King's sense of his call empowered him to stand under unsurmountable hardships. What empowers you to stand under hardship?

- King knew that speaking truth to power would cost him his life, yet he continued to speak. Would you continue to speak if speaking truth to power had the high cost of your life?

- Do you support the 12 principles that Dr. William Barber Poor People Campaign is founded on? For more information, check out:
https://www.poorpeoplescampaign.org/about/our-principles/

ABOUT THE AUTHOR

Colonel (Retired) David M. Lockhart is a native of Harvest, Alabama. He holds a Bachelor of Science degree in Political Science from Athens States College, Athens, Alabama; a Master of Divinity degree from Memphis Theological Seminary, Memphis, Tennessee; A Master's in Strategic Studies from the United States Army War College, Carlisle, Pennsylvania. He is currently a student at Wesley Theological Seminary in Washington, D. C. pursuing a Doctor of Ministry in Military Chaplaincy. He was ordained in 1991 by The Cumberland Presbyterian Church in America and served as Pastor for Mount Tabor Cumberland Presbyterian Church in Jackson, TN for four years. Of the many titles David has been called over the years, David is most honored to be called a servant leader and mentor. His passion is paying forward all the knowledge and open doors afforded to him on his journey through life.

"Everybody can be great...because anybody can serve. You don't have to have a college degree to serve. You don't have to make your subject and verb agree to serve. You only need a heart full of grace. A soul generated by love."

-Dr. Martin Luther King, Jr.

ACKNOWLEDGMENTS

There is an old African Proverb that says, *"If you want to go fast, go alone. If you want to go far, go together."* My success and accomplishments are due to the love, support, tutelage, and hard work of my family, friends, and supporters. To each of you, I say, *"Thank you. I truly would not have made it this far without you."*

"Rarely do we find men who willingly engage in hard, solid thinking. There is an almost universal quest for easy answers and half-baked solutions. Nothing pains some people more than having to think."

-Dr. Martin Luther King, Jr.

BIBLIOGRAPHY

1. Clayborne Carson, *The Autobiography of Martin Luther King, Jr.* (New York: Grand Central Publishing, 1998), 8, Kindle Edition.
2. Charles Marsh, *The Beloved Community: How Faith Shapes Social Justice from the Civil Rights Movement to Today* (New York: Basic Books), 11, Kindle Edition.
3. Martin Luther King, Jr., *Strive toward Freedom: The Montgomery Story* (Boston: Beacon Press), 9, Kindle Edition.
4. Ibid., 1352, Kindle Edition.
5. Drew D. Hansen, *The Dream: Martin Luther King, Jr., and the Speech That Inspired a Nation* (New York: HarperCollins Publishers), 6.
6. Hansen, *The Dream: Martin Luther King, Jr., and the Speech That Inspired a Nation.*
7. Charles Marsh, *The Beloved Community: How Faith Shapes Social Justice from the Civil Rights Movement to Today* (New York: Basic Books), 11, Kindle Edition.

8. Martin Luther King, Jr., *Strive toward Freedom: The Montgomery Story* (Boston: Beacon Press), 413–414, Kindle Edition.
9. Ibid., 825, *Strive toward Freedom: The Montgomery Story.*
10. Ibid., 861.
11. Ibid., 873–876.
12. Ibid., 876.
13. Ibid., 334.
14. Ibid., 494.
15. Ibid., 519.
16. Ibid., 627.
17. Ibid., 633.
18. Ibid., 686.
19. Ibid., 814.
20. Ibid., 825–826.
21. Ibid., 825.
22. Ibid., 1340.
23. Ibid., 1341.
24. Ibid., 1318–1322.
25. Ibid., 1340.
26. Ibid., 1419.
27. Ibid., 1420.
28. Ibid., 1427.
29. Ibid., 1435.
30. Ibid., 1446.
31. Ibid., 619
32. Ibid, 216
33. Ibid., 2248.

34. Lewis V. Baldwin, *To Make the Wounded Whole: The Cultural Legacy of Martin Luther King, Jr.* (Minneapolis: Fortress Press), 2280, Kindle Edition.
35. *To Make the Wounded Whole: The Cultural Legacy of Martin Luther King, Jr.*, 2666.
36. Ibid., 2669.
37. Michael Eric Dyson, *I May Not Get There with You: The True Martin Luther King, Jr.* (New York: The Free Press), 2000, 302.
38. Charles Marsh. *The Beloved Community: How Faith Shapes Social Justice from the Civil Rights Movement to Today* (New York: Basic Books), 128, Kindle Edition.
39. Ibid., 642.
40. Chuck Fager. *Uncertain Resurrection Dr. King's Poor Peoples Campaign-1968* (KIMO Press), 5

"If you can't fly then run, if you can't run then walk, if you can't walk then crawl, but whatever you do you have to keep moving forward."

-Dr. Martin Luther King, Jr.

STAY CONNECTED

Thank you for reading, *Table Talk Series Volume Two: Dr. Martin Luther King, Jr., The Prophet of Love*. David looks forward to connecting with you and keeping you updated on his next releases.

EMAIL lockedin333@gmail.com
INSTAGRAM Lockedin333
TWITTER @lockedin3332020
LINKEDIN David M. Lockhart

Made in the USA
Columbia, SC
01 October 2024